My Skateboard

Written by Maoliosa Kelly

Photographs by Steve Lumb

Collins

My pads.

My helmet.

My skateboard.

My friends.

My turn.

Yes!

13

Ideas for guided reading

Learning objectives: recounting the main points in the correct sequence; hearing and identifying initial sounds in words; reading high frequency words on sight. Recognising and discussing feelings.

Curriculum links: Physical development: Move with control and co-ordination; Personal, Social and Emotional Development: Be confident to try new activities.

High frequency words: my.

Interest words: pads, skateboard, helmet, friends, turn.

Word count: 11

Resources: two small card strips for each child.

Getting started

- Look at the front cover together. Discuss what the book might be about. Read the title.

- Walk through the book, looking at the pictures. Leave pp14-15 to explore later. Discuss what happens. *This boy enjoys skateboarding.* Ask the children what they enjoy doing.

- Ask them to find the word 'my' on each page. *What sound does this word begin with?*

- Ask the children what the boy does first, next and at the end. *What does he feel like on p11 when it is his turn?*

Reading and responding

- Read the book together from the beginning. As the children read, prompt and praise correct matching of spoken and written words particularly correct reading of the word *my*.

- Ask them to find words on the page (skateboard, helmet and pads). How did they find it? (I looked for a word beginning with 's'.)

- When you've read the book, look at pp14-15. Discuss with the children whether the skateboard jump was a new experience for the boy. *How did the boy feel before the jump? How did he feel when he had finished jumping?*

- Discuss the sequence of the book. Ask children to say in their own words what happened,' first', 'next' and 'in the end'.